Living Life In Short Chapters

Doc Irwin

Published by Doc Irwin, 2024.

LIVING LIFE IN SHORT CHAPTERS

First edition. October 4, 2024.

ISBN: 979-8227520654

Written by Doc Irwin.

Table of Contents

(1) 1
(2) 2
(3) 3
(4) 4
(5) 5
(6) 6
(7) 7
(8) 8
(9) 9
(10) 10
(11) 11
(12) 12
(13) 13
(14) 14
(15) 15
(16) 16
(17) 17
(18) 18
(19) 19
(20) 20
(21) 21
(22) 22
(23) 23
(24) 24
(25) 25
(26) 26
(27) 27
(28) 28
(29) 29
(30) 30
(31) 31

(32) 32
(33) 33
(34) 34
(35) 35
(36) 36
(37) 37
(38) 38
(39) 39
(40) 40
(41) 41
(42) 42
(43) 43
(44) 44
(45) 45
(46) 46
(47) 47
(48) 48
(49) 49
About Doc Irwin 50
Other Books by Doc Irwin 52

Dedicated to my wife and daughter who have supported me throughout this long process.

A Note from The Author

What follows is a memoir in journal format written about my 20-year battle against prostate cancer.

In it I've made an attempt to find a bit of dark humour in the day-to-day challenges that I've faced.

It was written over the last few years while I was trying to accept the fact that the treatment for this problem is going to remain with me for the remainder of my life.

The title "Living Life in Short Chapters" refers to the every 3-month injection and blood work I get, and the follow-up appointment that determines whether the treatment I'm getting is still working or needs to be changed.

(1)

I've seen the equation Comedy = Tragedy + Time, which, by the way, never appeared in any of the texts I used during my career as a math teacher. However, this equation, whether true or not, has been explored by Chuck Lorrie who wrote "According to the rules of comedy, your suffering will be funny after an undetermined length of time.".

Now I've tried to use this adage in my book "Looking Back ..... The Ramblings of Doc Irwin" when writing about certain events in my life. The story of my falling off a ladder and the subsequent tale of my heart attack and triple bypass became a humorous story ..... but only because I survived and was able to view the event and all the related occurrences from a relatively safe distance.

But now I've decided to write about another event in my life and see if any humour develops as I venture into the story. I'm actually not sure if this is going to work, because even though the story began over 20 years ago it is still ongoing ......and I'm not sure enough time has elapsed. But this is a start.

(2)

It all began just before Labour Day in 2003, when I visited my doctor for my annual physical. Everything seemed to be okay until he read the results of the PSA test. The number was high, so he suggested a biopsy at Princess Margaret Hospital. And at this point I regretted having missed the 'annual' the year before, but convinced myself that the number was probably an anomaly and casually called the hospital for an appointment. They told me that they had just had a cancellation for the following Tuesday so I decided to take it and just get the job done.

(3)

When Tuesday came, my wife and I decided that opening day for a class of Kindergarten kids was a big deal and that it would be very confusing if their teacher was not there on the first day. So, while my wife set out for school, I hopped on the subway and headed down to the hospital by myself anticipating a quick in and out, so to speak. Well...... it wasn't exactly what I was expecting, and as I lay there in the little recovery room, I cursed myself for not driving to the hospital. My penchant for saving money sometimes lands me in awkward situations .... and the amount saved by not driving and parking downtown was of small consolation at this point. But that's the fix I was in. The walk down to the subway, where I waited for the train to arrive, followed by subway rides on lines 1 and 2, and then boarding a bus and walking a couple of blocks home is something I'd rather forget. So, let's head into chapter 4.

(4)

Now the waiting game began. I had only waited 4 or 5 days for the biopsy but the results seemed to take forever to come back. But finally, after a few weeks I got a call to come in to my doctor's office. The fact that he wanted to deliver the news in person did not bode well. So, when I went in for the results, I was expecting the worst and that's exactly what I got. It was, however, a shocker in that I felt I had always taken good care of myself with very little alcohol consumed, 3 squares a day, and my only vice being that I had smoked a pipe for a few years when I was much younger.

But there it was. Not only were there cancerous cells in the sample but the Gleason Score, which tracks how aggressive the cancer is, was in the high range. It was kind of ironic that the term Gleason popped up because I had spent many happy hours in my youth watching the Jackie Gleason Show and listening to his orchestra fronted by Bobbie Hackett on trumpet. But that was the situation, a Gleason score indicating an active aggressive form of cancer and I felt like I had just been hit by a truck.

(5)

The meeting with Dr. G, the oncologist to whom I had been referred, took place on a dull, rainy day. It was as if mother nature had decided to give the occasion the solemnity it deserved. I remember looking out of the window in Dr. G's office observing the mist hanging over University Avenue as she read information from what I think was called a PalmPilot. I remember her speaking quietly and uttering the phrase "mean life expectancy 2 years" and my brain immediately latched onto those words. If my sense of humour had been intact, I would have asked what the standard deviation was .... as if a mean of 2 could have a deviation on 15 or 20. But all I could think of was that my daughter was only 12 and I needed more time. I had no idea that Dr. G meant 2 years without treatment and like an idiot I didn't ask for details. I was in a bad place in my head and just wanted to get the heck out of there.

(6)

The next appointment was with a surgeon who specialized in this type of problem. Once again it seemed to take forever until we met with him and when the day finally came the news was not good. Apparently, the biopsy indicated that the cancer had gone outside the prostate so removal was not the best option. I understood that there was a chance that this was not the case but the surgeon felt that radiation was the better option. So, after worrying about what could go wrong with an operation, I now had to focus my concern on all the preparations for radiation treatment. (I should let you know, at this point, that my natural state is to be worried about something so when one thing is resolved I have to find something else to worry about.) Part of this preparation for radiation involved creating a contour map of my insides and a very helpful nurse who knew I had a math/physics background explained the process to me. It reminded me of a geology course I had taken during my student days when I struggled to understand topographic maps and I hoped the doctors were better at reading them than I had been.

(7)

There were scans and various meetings over the next few weeks and we (whenever I say we, I mean my wife and I) met with the oncologist again. She immediately began talking about the radiation process and when my wife raised the question about the result of the scans the response was a curt "If there had been any problem discovered by the scans, I would have mentioned them to you when you arrived.".

It seemed like a harsh response and both of us felt intimidated by her direct manner and no-nonsense approach ... not exactly the hand-holding soft manner we were hoping for. But as it turned out, she was just what I needed and I soon learned that she was one of the top doctors in the entire world studying this field. So, although we were initially put off by, what might be called, her lack of 'bedside manner' our opinion soon changed.

Not long after, she saw me sitting alone in the cafeteria, waiting for a radiation appointment, and she came over and asked me how I was doing. And at this point I became aware of her softer side and realized that when she was dealing with life and death decisions on a daily basis, she had to be somewhat detached when analyzing the data.

(8)

It's impossible to write about radiation of the prostate without talking about the bowl and bladder. So here goes.

To get a clear view of the prostate, you need an empty bowel and a full bladder. And on one occasion while the technicians were doing the mapping that I talked about earlier, I was told that I should try to empty my bowel a little more. So, I headed into a washroom and emerged a few minutes later totally embarrassed with the news that unfortunately both had emptied. Apparently, this is a common occurrence and they just handed me a large container of water and said they'd try the procedure again in about half an hour.

The timing worked out okay but the amount of water I had consumed was almost beyond my capacity and when the procedure was over and they told me to get up off of the hard surface I had been lying on, I had a request. I suggested that they locate a bed pan and let me use it before I moved or they were going to need a mop and a bucket. My request was granted and they all got a chuckle when everything turned out okay.

(9)

I kept notes of all the appointments and procedures, including dates and times, but during one of the periodic cleanses of my desk I must have tossed them in a blue bin figuring I'd put it all behind me. So, now that I've made the decision to recall all this 'stuff' I have to guess at some of the timing.

I do remember though, that the radiation treatments started just before Christmas ... almost 3 months after all this nonsense began. I was to receive 42 treatments at the rate of 5 per week (weekends off) and I got Christmas Day off too. (That was a real fun Christmas.) Can't remember about New Year's Day.

The regimen involved taking a laxative at night and consuming a large amount of water in the morning. Each day I was given a specific time for a machine in the radiation department on the bottom floor of the hospital and to help me with my timing I decided to take the subway. The Queen's Park exit is right near the hospital so as long as there were no delays on the tube, I could get there close to my scheduled time.

(10)

Drinking copious amounts of water while riding the subway and then discovering that the machine you are scheduled for is 45 minutes behind can lead to some rather uncomfortable situations. So, I had to modify my plan. Instead of trying to arrive right on time I tried to arrive about 45 minutes early and check to see if the machine was on schedule. Then I'd go up to the 5th floor where there was some sort of cafeteria area and I sat there and drank my water while looking out onto University Avenue. (This is where Dr. G discovered me and chatted for a while.)

One of the students I was tutoring had given me a small radio for Christmas and I tried to listen to Jazz 91FM, although the reception in the building wasn't that great. And then, when it was close to the appointment time I headed down to the basement.

Actually, when I told some of the other patients what I was doing they decided to come early too and drink their water at the hospital. Even though it wasn't exactly the best of times for me it felt good that I had helped a few people to manage the situation better.

(11)

The actual experience in the radiation room wasn't painful in any way. I had to lie down on a flat surface, facing the ceiling and a nurse would line up the machine with the tattoos on my body. Oh yes, the tattoos. I forgot to mention earlier that they tattooed a dot on each side of my body and one on the front to line up the machine so that the radiation was directed at the right spot. Sometimes they used a magic marker to circle the tiny dots to make them easier to find. I recall that on a few occasions the nurse tried to remove the smudged marker circle on the front of my body with a solution of some kind and redraw the circle. I had to remind her that too much pressure could result in a 'problem' .... After all, my bladder was barely holding on at this point.

Then, as soon as everything was lined up, the nurse left the room, closed the door, and I was on my own. Occasionally someone would come back in to move me slightly and then leave again. Soon after, the machine started up and it was show- time.

(12)

The radiation machine had a rhythm to it, moving in a semi-circle about 3 feet over top of me. Every few seconds it would stop and do whatever it does to shoot the rays into my body. Sometimes I would try to imagine the rays hitting the target but there was really no sensation from it. Also, after a few days of this I could anticipate where the apparatus was going to stop, and knew exactly how many stops there were on its journey over and back to where it started.

A nurse told me about a little boy who had been positioned on this machine a few months before. After she had left the room and was ready to start the process she noticed on her screen (they do watch you from the outside) that the room was empty. Apparently, the poor little guy had decided this was not for him and escaped out a rear door. I really understood the terror he must have sensed and felt very lucky to have made it to 59 years of age before encountering a situation like this.

<h1 style="text-align:center">(13)</h1>

I must tell you about the music. That's the one thing I'll never forgot. It's often said that a song can immediately carry you back to a time and place where that song was played. And in my case, there are two singers that immediately put me back on the machine in the radiation room. The first is Tom Jones. For some reason I've never liked Tom Jones. In fact, hearing Delila, for me, is akin to a nail screeching across a chalk board. So, the fact that I had to listen to him in that situation was neither here nor there in terms of ruining any enjoyment for me.

However, the other singer is Nora Jones. I had always liked Nora Jones and the fact that hearing her now takes me back to that room is a darn shame. Sorry Nora, but that's just the way things turned out.

I've often thought over the years that if they were going to go with a 'Jones' theme they could have used a little imagination. A recording of Spike Jones and His City Slickers doing their bizarre recording of "Cocktails For Two" would have passed the time in a more uplifting way.

(14)

As soon as I was released from the radiation room, retrieved my clothes, and of course used a nearby washroom, I was free to go. And since there were no after effects of the procedure I headed for the subway. I almost felt guilty being able to escape in this manner because I got to know a few patients who had other cancers and their treatment had unfortunate side effects. One of these fellows had a type of throat cancer and between the cancer and the radiation he had lost the ability to eat solid food and anything he consumed had to be taken in through a straw. Others were from out of the city and stayed in a residence near the hospital.

I, on the other hand, got to pretend that nothing out of the ordinary was going on and went back to my regular life. Since I was working as a math tutor at the time, on some of these days I was able to get to a High School by noon and work through a lunch period as well as having a few more sessions after school and in the evening. It helped immensely to be able to pretend that everything was okay.

(15)

But everything wasn't okay. I guess you can hide all the bad feelings and thoughts somewhere in your head for a while, but eventually they bust out of whatever bag you've stuffed them into.

In my case it was on a Sunday afternoon, about half way through the 42 sessions, when it all came tumbling down and I had to admit to myself that this wasn't easy. It seemed like I just hit a wall at this point and had to remind myself "I've got cancer and all the optimism in the world isn't going to fix it and if these sessions at the hospital don't work it's game over".

So, the mess inside me all came tumbling out and I had my day of feeling sorry for myself. Then after that stormy day came to an end, I decided to try to balance my feelings with what I felt was realism mixed with optimism. Some days would be okay and some not okay. And on the not okay days I would have to believe that the next day would be better.

(16)

I mentioned earlier about a young boy 'escaping' out the back door of one of the rooms housing a radiation machine. And it reminded me of a few incidents while I was sitting around waiting for my turn.

There was a children's hospital nearby and occasionally a nurse would bring a small child in a wheel chair into the waiting room.

Now this wasn't exactly a happy place to be, but I always tried to keep my emotions in check. However, it was hard to hold back the tears when a young boy or girl was wheeled into the room. My heart went out to someone so young that had to face a situation like this.

(17)

Eventually Day 42 arrived .... the day of my last visit to the radiation department. It had been a long haul, spanning about 8 weeks, and I felt that there should be something to mark the occasion....not that I expected a cake and balloons or a big card wishing me a fond goodbye. But all I can remember from that day is putting my clothes back on, dumping my hospital gown into a bin and heading out to the Queen's Park Subway Station. As I made my way home for the last time....well, the last time for this part of the process, I kept wondering if the radiation had worked and if so, how well. Did it stop the cancer dead in its tracks or just slow it down? Only time would tell.

(18)

So, now I'm going back to that day in September when the journey started. My family doctor had given me a prescription for casodex which is a drug used to lower the PSA number. Although this seemed to be a positive step, my oncologist was not happy with the situation since it would give a false reading when she took another blood test. However, over the long haul it was going to be a series of hormonal pills and injections that would play the major part in treating this disease.

(19)

It's been over a month since I wrote the last chapter because hormonal treatment has certain consequences and I wasn't sure if I was ready to

....

(20)

After another pause, I'm back again and I've decided to start the hormonal talk with a humorous story from my youth.

When I was in High School, I took a music listening course. During one of the classes the teacher talked about the Castrati, who were male singers whose voices were equivalent to that of a soprano. This was accomplished by an operation when they were young. One of my friends, who was always looking for trouble, asked if the 'operation' was on their throat. This brought a curt "NO" from the teacher who quickly changed the topic. So ...... although this was only one of my concerns, I asked the doctor if the treatment, which is a sort of hormonal castration, would affect my voice and was told that it would not. Although this was a relief, as time went on, I realized that it was only a small victory in what was to be a journey that I will only describe now as being 'interesting and challenging'.

(21)

Although my voice didn't change something else did. And it was embarrassing. Because my chest began to develop breasts. Back then I used to run occasionally .... not far and not really run ... more of a jog .... and that's when I noticed them. At first it was just kind of funny but as time went on it became annoying. So, I stopped jogging.

(22)

The other problem with the developing breast situation was that they hurt.... not all the time, but whenever anything bumped into them. It didn't have to be much. Even putting a jacket on could hurt. And the act of crossing my arms on my chest soon became a thing of the past. The worst was when I had to have an echo cardiogram because the contraption they use had to be pressed down hard in that area. It was definitely a new experience, but a small price to pay if this treatment kept me alive.

(23)

So far, I've written about my voice not changing and something else that did change but I've avoided the biggest problem of all. And that's the fact that hormonal treatment plays with your emotions. I had always been someone who, as the old saying goes, wore his emotions on his sleeve but this was ridiculous. Not only the feeling of despair and wanting to cry a lot but there were the hot flashes too. I wasn't exactly feeling like the 'tough guy' image I wanted to portray through all this. Usually, it was the worst in the morning so getting out and being active helped. But it was a really tough thing to manage.

(24)

I've seen ads where older men are encouraged to take a supplement to increase testosterone .... not just for sex, but to increase their zest for life and their desire to be active and creative. But when you're taking a drug that reduces testosterone to zero so that cancer cells have nothing to feed on, you have to do a lot of self talk and use your mind to lift you up. And that was a new skill I had to learn.

People often confuse the order of creativity and motivation .... waiting for motivation before acting. But the fact is that by acting first, motivation follows. By setting goals and trying to be creative I gave myself a feeling of self worth and that I was still okay.

(25)

I'm not saying it was easy, but with the support of my family I pressed on. In addition to tutoring I began writing math support books and within a few years I had written about nine books. And thanks to a friend who offered them for sale at his retail stores, one of them even got 'Best Seller' status. Not that this solved the problems I was facing but it sure helped by giving me something to focus on.

(26)

The main problem for me is the uncertainty, because every 84 days I have to have a blood test and see the oncologist. I get stressed before each of the meetings and feel the weight of it all on my shoulders as we head down to the hospital for the meeting. Is the treatment working? What will the PSA number be? Has it gone up again? Will they have to take more scans to see if the cancer has spread? All of these questions swirling around in my mind.

And after the meeting .... maybe an appointment for a scan or another drug to add but usually a sigh of relief after hearing we're staying the course and they'll see me in 3 months.

It's like living life in short chapters.

(27)

Okay, okay. I've accepted the new additions to my chest, the hot flashes, the lack of testosterone, the mood swings and all that but now... you've got to be kidding. The hormones have affected my bones and now I'm going for periodic bone density tests and I've officially got osteoporosis. (Thank goodness I have spell check or the spelling of osteoporosis would have been a disaster.) But seriously, I want to have a talk with whoever wrote the script for my life.

<h1 align="center">(28)</h1>

On one of my visits to the oncologist .... Oh, by the way, I usually didn't visit the actual oncologist assigned to my case but rather a colleague or intern. Anyway, on this particular occasion I was given the option of a different drug. This one would be every 4 months rather that 3 months ..... meaning slightly longer chapters in my life story. So, I decided to try it.

This one was injected somewhere in my rear end rather than the first one which got poked into my stomach. Intramuscular I think they said. However, when I went to get out of bed the next morning the muscle they hit was so sore I could hardly walk. I tried it again 4 months later with the same result so we went back to drug number one.

(29)

I almost forgot to tell you about the needle. One time when the regular nurse in the oncology department was away, two nurses came into the room. And as I lay there, facing the ceiling, one leg bent, I heard one say to the other "I've never seen a needle that large!" Needless to say, it wasn't exactly what I wanted to hear at the moment. Many years later, at my local doctor's office, I mentioned this to the nurse who was giving me the shot and she told me that her reaction had been the same. She had never seen a needle that large. Apparently, unlike a regular type of needle, this one has a large bore that delivers a time release capsule under the skin. All I know is that it just hurts for a brief moment but within a few days leaves a little rainbow of yellow and purple colours on my stomach.

As for the actual size of the needle .... I have no idea, because I just lie there focussing on the ceiling.

(30)

I wouldn't recommend it but I was able to forget about cancer for a while by falling off a ladder onto a cement garage floor...... breaking my right femur..... and having a heart attack somewhere along the way. After a triple bi-pass and a 5 week stay in the hospital and a rehab centre I resumed life at home again. I wouldn't suggest any similar action for anyone else in order to get out of worrying about cancer ......but it sure worked for me.

(31)

Some days I feel like a fraud, because I see other people that are going through the agony of chemotherapy ... feeling sick, lacking energy, sometimes bed ridden .... and here I am going about my day as if nothing was wrong. But the fact that I have cancer cells in my body is hard to forget about and I just wish there was a cure, rather than living with this for the rest of my life.

(32)

For about 15 years, every 84 days or so, I got on the subway and travelled down to the hospital and spent an hour or so in the huge waiting room outside the lab. It was always an education for me as I observed all the different people waiting for a blood test. It was a complete cross-section of humanity ... young, middle aged, old, some looking frail with kerchiefs hiding bald heads, others looking the picture of health. Sometimes I had a conversation with someone beside me but most of the time I just waited quietly. Occasionally, if my number was about 50 away from the number on the big red sign, I would get a coffee at the Tim's inside the hospital and go for a walk on University Avenue. If the weather was okay, I'd sit on the little wall at the edge of the sidewalk and watch the bustle of the real world outside the hospital.

(33)

While waiting at the hospital lab, I'd go to the pharmacy to give them my prescription for the medication to be picked up the next week. The lady who was usually working at the counter was very kind and friendly and as the years went on, I looked forward to seeing her there. The anxiety I felt was always helped by her calm manner and I was quite disappointed when I learned that she had retired and was no longer working there.

It was F. Scott Fitzgerald that wrote "It was only a sunny smile, and little it cost in the giving, but like morning light it scattered the night and made the day worth living."

It's amazing how a small interaction like that can be so important.

(34)

Many times when I entered the hospital there would be a desk where you could buy lottery tickets. I'm not a fan of lotteries but by buying these tickets it was a way to support the research at the hospital. And so, I occasionally decided to dig deep and come up with the $100 for a ticket. My rational for doing this was two-fold. Firstly, I was getting thousands of dollars worth of treatment and was required to pay absolutely nothing for it...... so it was a way of giving a little back. The second thing in my mind was that, having had the bad luck of getting this disease, I should have a counter balance of good luck by winning the lottery. Apparently, that was faulty reasoning on my part and as a former teacher of probability I should have known better..... but I'm glad I donated the money.

(35)

Since I had lived and worked in the 'burbs' all my life I rarely needed to ride on the subway. So, the 42 round trips to and from the hospital for radiation and subsequent trips for appointments caused me to associate the subway with dealing with cancer. I must have heard the 'closing the door chimes' a thousand times during these trips.

I once saw an article about the different sounds that subways around the world make when the doors are closing. The description of our city's chimes (that eventually kept rattling around in my brain) was that it was a downward arpeggio. However, I kept thinking it was the opening notes of 'A Bicycle Built For Two' and I had to finish the song in my head…. anything to keep my mind on something other than why I was there.

(36)

Whenever I have a meeting with a representative of the team that is looking after my case, my wife and I drive downtown to the hospital. There's a large parking building behind the hospital and usually after entering, we circle from floor to floor looking for a place to park. On most visits we figure that at $5 per half hour we use up the first $5 trying to find a spot to park. That remark was supposed to be funny but the circling around, seeing all the cars belonging to other patients just adds to the stress I usually feel on 'visitation day'.

(37)

Sitting in the waiting room at the hospital I look at all the other guys waiting to see an oncologist. I was only 59 years old when I first sat in that room and all the other patients seemed so much older than I was. I kept thinking "Lucky me, getting this at such a young age". But now after 19 years of this I fit right in. It's not exactly a fun club to belong to, but at least I'm still alive.

(38)

Today was another 'visit to the lab day'. Ever since Covid restrictions entered our lives I've been going to a local lab for my blood test. In a way it's better because it allows me to pretend that it's just a regular blood test for my GP and not connected to the disease I'm trying to keep at bay. The lab was crowded, so after I checked in at the desk, I stood outside in the hall, leaning against the wall reading 'Breakfast of Champions' by Kurt Vonnegut. I like Vonnegut's writing because he had such a weird sense of humour .... the kind of bizarre view of life I rely on to get through many of my days.

(39)

After many years of hormone shots and the side effects, I sometimes wish I had been afflicted with a cancer that could have been attacked vigorously with chemo so that I could one day be 'in remission' or cancer free. I have a former classmate from High School who has cancer and keeps updating his friends via e-mail with the various treatments he's receiving. At first, I was envious of the fact that he had a chance to beat the disease and leave it behind, but lately things have not gone so well for him. Nausea, severe weight loss, and lack of energy are dragging him down and the cancer is spreading. I'm now thinking of the old saying "be careful what you wish for" and although I'll never be able to say I'm cancer free, my day-to-day life is good and I'm grateful for that.

(40)

During visits to the hospital, we wait in a large room until my name is called. Then we wait in a smaller room. In the large room there are windows and lots of people to watch. For a few years there was also a TV screen with the news repeating over and over and over. But in the little room there is only a computer with the hospital network logo on it and a few signs posted on the walls.

Every time I'm in the little room I think of an old TV show featuring the British comedian, Tony Hancock. An entire episode took place in a doctor's waiting room with Mr. Hancock trying to occupy his time with all kinds of ridiculous activities. At one point he reads a sign and keeps repeating "Drink a pint o' milk a day. Drink a pint o' milk a day. Drink a pint o' milk a day." And, he eventually starts singing "Coughs and Sneezes Spread Diseases" to the melody of the German National Anthem. The memory of that show helps me pass the time and realize that many people have the same reaction to waiting for appointments and that the silliness of reading a sign over and over is a universal act of desperation.

(41)

I guess it's time that I wrote about the elephant in the room. By that I mean the effect that hormone drugs have on one's sexuality. But the truth is that it's no walk in the park. I'm not prepared to discuss any of that and if you're going through this process or just wonder about what it's like you'll have to find another book.... Or look it up somewhere on the interweb.... because I'm ducking the question completely. So there.

(42)

Today I had to go for a stress test. My oncologist once told me that I'd probably die of something other than cancer because I was 'responding so well' to the treatment. So, here's something else to worry about. Actually, a stress test isn't that bad .... the only painful part is the pressure on my chest during the echocardiogram. If you were paying attention, you'll remember the tenderness caused by the growth spurt in the breast region. It's somewhat better now but as Duke Ellington wrote, "Things Ain't What They Used To Be".

(43)

Another 3-month chapter of my life is coming to an end tomorrow when I meet with my oncologist to get the results of the latest blood test. Kind of a busy week in that I had my usual injection today as well. The highlight of the visit this afternoon was the fact that the nurse had to really press to get the needle in. She apologized for the pain although it wasn't really her fault. I guess that after years of injections in my gut there is a fair bit of scar tissue built up and it's hard to find a new spot anymore. But it's a small price to pay in order to stay alive.

(44)

I can't remember if I told you but after being under her care for about 18 years, my original oncologist retired and I've been bouncing around with various interns since then. I met my new oncologist today …. seems like a nice guy …. easy to understand and he explained my options well. PSA is stable so we decided on 'steady as she goes' and we'll meet again, this time in 4 months. It was left up to me to keep track and stay on the 84-day injection regime I've been on since what feels like the beginning of time. The meeting was kind of interesting in that he indicated that I'm kind of an anomaly. The biopsy almost 20 years ago indicated that the cancer was quite aggressive but the radiation and hormone injections seem to have caused it to remain fairly benign in the prostate. I've always been fearful that it would suddenly flare up and travel to new locations but the doc figures I'll be okay if we just keep doing what we've been doing. And that something else will probably kill me first …. Not sure I like to think about that but we all have to go sometime.

(45)

There's not a lot of humour on a cancer journey, but a few years ago I was at a party for some former teachers I'd worked with. And I ended up talking to a friend who was on the same journey as I was. He remarked that my skin was so smooth .... that I kept looking younger every time he saw me. The fact that he's gay gave this comment an added dimension. He then totally broke me up when he suggested that it was probably the drug my cancer doctor was giving me and he wistfully suggested that maybe he'd ask his oncologist if he could give him the same one. It may not sound that funny to you, but I remember that we both broke up laughing .... laughing that a drug given to help us live a few extra years could actually make us look younger.

(46)

After almost 20 years of treatment, I thought that I knew my way around the hospital fairly well. But the last time I went for a meeting we got totally lost. There was a sign outside the room where I had always gone explaining how to get to the new location but somehow, we got totally disorientated in the bowels of the building searching for a way back to civilization. And since I hate being late for any appointment, I was totally flustered by the time we found someone (and believe me, we asked quite a few) who had any idea where we were supposed to be. The ridiculous part of this was the fact that we then waited about 20 minutes before we were sent to a consultation room and then at least 45 more minutes for the doctor to arrive. And I never seem to learn because I always arrive on time and I always wait seemingly forever to see someone.

(47)

Every once in a while, things go off the rails .... like today. I had called my local pharmacy last week to pick up my usual injection and was told that they didn't have any refill instructions left. So, they would have to fax the hospital. Seemed simple enough but today when I called to see if the prescription had been filled, I was told that they couldn't get the fax to go through. So .... I tried all the phone numbers I've used over the years without success and finally tried the general number for the department and left what I thought was a clear and thoughtful message. However, the message they left when they called back (of course I was out when they called) was to see if my pharmacy had any refill instructions .... which meant that my message had been totally misinterpreted and I was right back where I started.

After much stress and gnashing of teeth I finally got a fax number for the drug store. But I wasted the better part of an afternoon getting to this point and still don't know if the problem is solved. You'd think that at this advanced age I wouldn't get stressed over stuff like this .... but I still haven't learned.

(48)

Well .....that's about it for now. Going for about my 100th blood test today .... wondering how long I'll have to wait this time. I was going to try to make it to chapter 50 but there doesn't seem to be anything else to say. And I don't have any words of wisdom to wind up this story .... been kind of a conversation with myself ..... looking back over the whole journey. Maybe I'll share this with other people some day but for now it'll be tucked away in my computer in the folder labelled 'stuff'.

(49)

I'm back again .... writing this after a break of a couple of months ..... and I wanted to say that the worst part of this journey for me is the constant reminder of how fragile life is. It would be so much more pleasant to go for more than 3 months just enjoying being alive without the constant reminder that something inside my body is trying to kill me. On the other hand, it's also a reminder of what a miracle life is and highlights how fortunate I am to still be alive.

Anyway, I finally decided to send this to a publisher. Hopefully my words will help a few people to not feel so alone in their journey. I'm very grateful for the twenty years that the hospital treatment plan has given me, but since there seems to be no end to my story, I'm just going to quit writing now. So that's all folks! Goodbye and good luck.

About Doc Irwin

About the Author/Publisher

'Doc Irwin' is the alter ego of a former teacher who spent 30 years teaching math as well as assisting in the music department after school. About five years into his retirement, during which he had continued working in the area of math as a private tutor, he was diagnosed with prostate cancer. The outlook was grim and in a desperate effort to stop worrying and fill his time with something positive, he began writing a series of Math Study Guides for High School students. The project continued for many years as 10 different guides were published. The Grade 9 book actually became a Best Seller in Canada.

However, around the age of 70, after writing about math problems, the author realized that in spite of his underwhelming achievements when he struggled with English in his youth, he actually enjoyed writing stories about his life. Hence 'Doc Irwin', the sidekick of the serious math guy was born, and story after story about his life came pouring out until there were enough for a book called "Looking Back ... The Ramblings of Doc Irwin".

But then another idea popped up. You see, the writing of the 'Doc Irwin' stories was a continuation of the attempted escape from the problem that had led to all this writing in the first place. So, the author finally decided to write about the elephant in the room. The elephant, meaning the prostate problem, could be confronted by writing about it. In the beginning there was no intent to publish any of these thoughts and feelings. But when a volunteer who had driven hundreds of people to appointments for cancer treatment was shown this journal, it was suggested that these writings could possibly help people in a similar situation.

So, in the preceding pages I've shared my day-by-day thoughts. And thanks to my friend and author, Mark Leslie, and the folks at Draft2Digital the book has become a reality.

Other Books by Doc Irwin

LOOKING BACK: **The Ramblings of Doc Irwin**
I definitely did not set out to write a book. Honest! That would have been shear madness. With a mark of 55% in my final High School English Course, I went straight into math and physics leaving the literary world to those who actually know how to spell. My logical mind is more suited to probing math problems than analysing prose. So this book's existence is pure serendipity.

After publishing 10 math books I started a Facebook page to create some interest in the guides. With two fingers and the help of spell-check, I began rambling on about math related stuff, but as I became more desperate for material the whole thing suddenly morphed into stories about my life. Then, about a year later, I had enough material to fill a book.

I have no illusions about the literary merit of what I've written. I've read some of these ramblings myself and find them to be written in a dull plodding style reminiscent of my math books but without the numbers. However by publishing this collection of thoughts I can spare my friends and family from constant repetition of these tales as I glide into senility. Even if they ask, I'll just say "read the book". (You're welcome!)

The stories are not organised in any particular way ...I thought about cataloging them in some fashion, but after 50 years of teaching math I'm so done with order and logic. It's highly overrated anyway. So here they are: true stories of actual events in my life (at least how I remember them)... random snippets from the life of a math teacher, wannabe jazz piano player, and occasional 's@#t disturber'.